HAL•LEONARD
INSTRUMENTAL PLAY-ALONG

AUDIO ACCESS INCLUDED

PLAYBACK+
Speed • Pitch • Balance • Loop

TRUMPET

PIRATES OF THE CARIBBEAN

To access audio visit:
www.halleonard.com/mylibrary

Enter Code
6638-7634-3320-3875

ISBN 978-1-4234-2199-3

WALT DISNEY MUSIC COMPANY

DISTRIBUTED BY

HAL•LEONARD®
CORPORATION

7777 W. BLUEMOUND RD. P.O. BOX 13819 MILWAUKEE, WI 53213

Visit Hal Leonard Online at
www.halleonard.com

Title	Page

THE BLACK PEARL

TRUMPET

Music by KLAUS BADELT

5

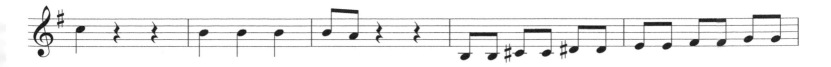

small notes optional

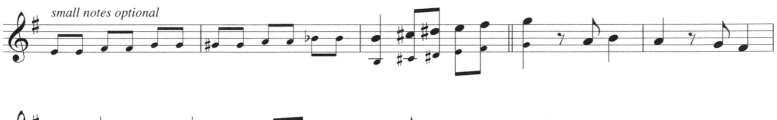

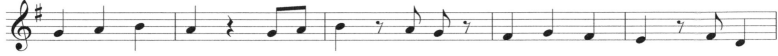

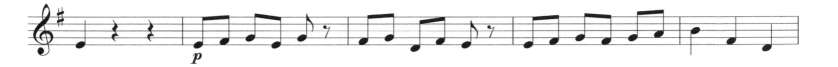

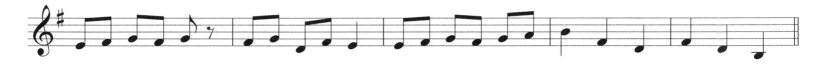

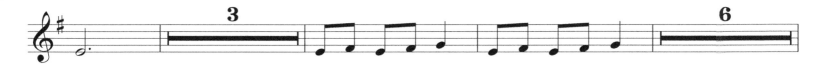

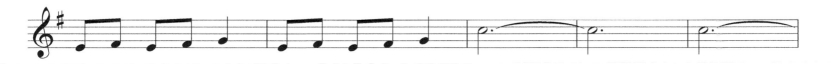

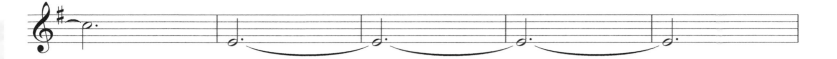

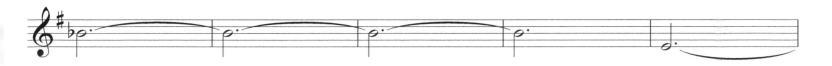

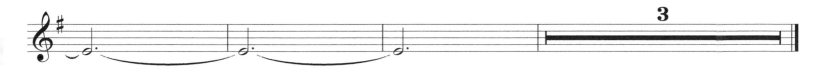

BLOOD RITUAL/
MOONLIGHT SERENADE

TRUMPET

Music by KLAUS BADELT

DAVY JONES PLAYS HIS ORGAN

TRUMPET

Music by HANS ZIMMER

DAVY JONES

Music by HANS ZIMMER

TRUMPET

DINNER IS SERVED

TRUMPET

Music by HANS ZIMMER

I'VE GOT MY EYE ON YOU

TRUMPET

Music by HANS ZIMMER

HE'S A PIRATE

TRUMPET

Music by KLAUS BADELT

13

JACK SPARROW

TRUMPET

Music by HANS ZIMMER

THE KRAKEN

TRUMPET

Music by HANS ZIMMER

THE MEDALLION CALLS

TRUMPET

Music by KLAUS BADELT

ONE LAST SHOT

TRUMPET

Music by KLAUS BADELT

TO THE PIRATE'S CAVE!

TRUMPET

Music by KLAUS BADELT

TWO HORNPIPES
(Fisher's Hornpipe)

TRUMPET

By SKIP HENDERSON

WHEEL OF FORTUNE

TRUMPET

Music by HANS ZIMMER

UNDERWATER MARCH

TRUMPET

Music by KLAUS BADELT